Rhona Warwick Paterson

SITE REPORT

A Theatrum Mundi Edition

Foreword P.5	A. Windows P.9
B. The Telling of the Tables P.27	C. The Sink is a Pore P.67

Cities
Writing
Culture
Infrastructure
Cultural Infrastructure
Urban Backstage
Domestic Space
Windows
Tables
Sink

I sit at my kitchen/dining table as I write these words. The kitchen/dining table is the sole species of the genus *table* in my home, with the exception of the so-called nesting tables that would more appropriately be classed as stools. They are useless for writing and their task is to provide support for house plants. Hence, the only table in the flat has no companions who speak *table* language to converse with. Her existence is silent and solitary, unlike that of the tables in Rhona Warwick Paterson's screenplay for six tables and three humans - 'The Telling of Tables' - included in this book.

From time to time I look out of the window in front of me, searching for words / searching for ideas / enjoying the view of a maple tree in its summer leaf covering the entire white frame. It feels as if I were writing in a treehouse. There is no street / no city visible beyond. I almost forget they are just below and beyond the tree. I hear cars passing, teenagers playing football in the playground; someone is dragging a suitcase, someone slams a car door, someone says hello to someone else. In my *treehouse*, I'm both in the city and removed from it.

I bring my gaze back from the bright green leaves, still in the hot afternoon air beyond the window, and look at the screen. My fingers type, and words appear in neat rows. They are flowing, which is a relief. The deadline is looming. The space temporarily filled with *Lorem ipsum dolor sit amet…* is awaiting them. A pipe underneath my sink gurgles as the dishwasher discharges dirty dishwater into it. I discharge further words onto the screen.

The roaring water behind me is not a distraction, a domestic interference invading my work. The sink just outside of my peripheral vision is key; it is the subject - one of three subjects - of this book I have the pleasure to be introducing to you.

Site Report by Rhona Warwick Paterson brings together a body of texts created during her fellowship at Theatrum Mundi, which began on 1 April 2020, following Rhona's contribution to the public programme titled *Homemade*, curated at Agile Cities in Glasgow in June 2019. This series of events coincided with the exhibition *Urban Backstages*, which presented a part of our larger project examining cultural infrastructure in London, Glasgow, Paris and Marseille, with a particular focus on places where culture is made - the urban backstage - rather than consumed - the urban onstage of museums, galleries, concert venues and theatres. *Homemade* focused on a then largely overlooked cultural infrastructure of domestic space where culture is conceived and produced. Rhona set out on the subsequent fellowship with an aim to explore how we inhabit and engage with domestic spaces as sites for the creative imagination. Little did she know, at the time of writing the proposal for her project in autumn 2019, that her world - and the world of most of us - would shrink to the territory of the domestic space, while at the same time her subject matter would gain a timely urgency and a broad audience.

Over the long months of 2020 and 2021, Rhona's imagination travelled the worlds of windows, tables and sinks. These elements of her domestic space became infrastructures for writing. The resulting *Site Report* is a collection of poetry in prose, verse and screenplay, where windows are a lot more than panes of glass, tables have minds of their own and sinks are conduits that connect to the wider world beyond the home.

Perhaps I write these words to you from my kitchen/living room, looking out of the window, listening to the sink behind me, because I am a woman writer/editor/producer and the kitchen/dining table is the default workspace for women in these professions, with only some of us enjoying a room of our own. Perhaps I write these words to you from within my domestic space because we have only just emerged from the Covid-19 pandemic and the domestic space is still the default workspace for many. In any case, on behalf of Theatrum Mundi, I invite you on a journey into the worlds of windows, tables and sinks that should never be reduced to their mere objecthood.

Marta Michalowska
Theatrum Mundi
June 2022

WINDOWS

I.   The Other [Half of the] World

On the front cover of Georges Perec's seminal collection of essays *Species of Spaces and Other Pieces*, originally published in 1974, Perec peers out at you from behind a set of French windows. He stands with his arms crossed, perhaps because he is outside in the cold or maybe he just feels awkward at having his photograph taken. His face, in contradiction to his body, holds an expression of quizzical mocking, of a schoolboy who has posed an impossible riddle, a proposition without an answer. Perec is smiling but remote – physically untouchable (on the outside-side of a window), yet his direct eye contact seems intimate and familiar. It is as if he were withholding a secret he desperately wants you to know. This is but one of the photograph's many contradictions.

On that day in 1978, the sky behind Georges has the appearance of a winter fog, a subject he refers to in his short story 'The Winter Journey', which looks at the temporal embodiment of poetry's atmospheric space in the physical world. His wondrous halo of frizzy dark hair is both consuming and being consumed by the milky exterior world. The view beyond the apartment window suggests he is on the top floor of the building where the tips of a few bare trees are just about visible, above them a tonal shift suggests a horizon line and a distance that speaks of open space and broad skies. Has Georges left the clutter of his Paris apartment to take up an offer of space and solitude to finish his book? An invitation, maybe, from a friend whose neglected family villa happens to be empty for the winter. Or had he recently read Joris-Karl Huysman's novel *Against Nature* (1884) and was intrigued by the protagonist, Jean des Esseintes, and his attempts to retreat from society in order to create his own world – an interior resolutely and decadently 'against the grain' of ordinary life. While the space of this particular reverie satisfies certain fantasies on the locus of the realm of imagination and revelation, Georges

seems more at home in the sparse dilapidation that pervades the image of this book cover.

The top of the photograph (partly obfuscated by the title of the book) reveals railings and a fragment of a window; now everything in this image is suddenly recategorised – the horizon line becomes a tonal shift on the wall of an internal courtyard and the crowns of trees are nothing more than mere light-seeking indoor plants. Technically, the skill required to photograph into the light (through a window) without losing important details in Perec's backlit face or the window frame through which the photograph is taken had to be significant, both in the set-up and in the darkroom afterwards. Perec at that time was a consummate exponent of riddles, games and word plays. The ludic literary devices he often employed were instrumental in drawing his readers into playful interactions with his own writing as an active reciprocity between reader and writer. The contradictions in this image prompt questions: Was this another of Perec's riddles?; Was his intention to ask the reader to enter into the space of writing or merely to interrogate what one sees and how one describes what we think we see?

I type the following phrases into my search engine:

>
> Perec front cover of Species of Spaces, a riddle?
> visual OuLiPian constraints
> shooting into light with stills camera, exposure time?
> Maurice Henry / L'Express, photographer, Perec
> Maurice Henry, Georges Perec
> Les archives de L'Express
> 1978

Nothing reveals itself – at least nothing that interrogates this image. The identity of the photographer, Maurice Henry, is attributed to *L'Express*, the French news magazine. My online searches reveal that Henry, a Paris resident, was a surrealist poet, photographer, painter and filmmaker who may well have known Perec through the OuLiPo group, a collective of writers and mathematicians who used constrained writing strategies. There is no official evidence of Henry working at the magazine though.

Eventually, I find a small reference in the online archives of *L'Express*. Following the success of Perec's *Life: A User's Manual* in 1978, the magazine sent the journalist Michel Bosquet to interview Perec for a feature piece. Bosquet was a pseudonym used by André Gorz – a philosopher, social critic, close friend of Jean-Paul Sartre and idiosyncratic commentator on the French left. Gorz was a significant figure in the student and worker protests in Paris in 1968 and subsequently, following the demise of the movement, became a flag-bearer for the fusion of socialist and ecological politics. As there are no digitised transcripts of this interview, I telephone the *L'Express* archives and speak to Pierre Getzler who sends me a scan of the published interview. Archived with this edition are Gorz's notes in shorthand from the interview with Perec that took place on the same day the photograph was taken. Getzler, now also intrigued by this photograph of Perec, arranges to have the shorthand notes translated into longhand. This piece of documentation has only now been made public and finally sheds some light on the peculiarity of this image.

Maurice Henry (MH) photographing George Perec (GP):

MH: I should like to photograph you in natural light. It won't take long.

[*GP agitated, looks to the window.*]

MH: Now… [*moving a desk chair*] if you could sit here next to the window… Don't look so scared Georges! Relax, enjoy the view, the light is perfectly overcast. Now, as you know, authors are at their best when looking out of a window, as if into the distance, in contemplation of the world outside.

GP: But the world outside this window holds no particular interest to me, Maurice. These authors you speak of… with their 'performing' of contemplation… It's so evidently a confection! Now tell me why I should conform to this inauthentic charade, for the purpose of 'good light', to make your job easy?

[*Much laughter. MH lights GP's cigarette and slaps him on the shoulder.*]

MH: Georges, Georges… Always questioning! Aren't you exhausted?

GP: My friend, it is such orthodoxies that make me exhausted! However, I have endless energy to question the desire for such spectacles… I ask you, will my contrived 'contemplation' sell more copies of the magazine? Back me up here André!

[*Notes stop here. It is assumed that André Gorz joins the discussion.*]

GP: What did those authors, with their affectations... their silly tobacco pipes, like your friend André, what's his name? [*laughter*] What did they see from their windows? What existential landscape were they contemplating?

MH: A dog taking a shit? [*laughter*]

GP: Aha, indeed, the shit – truly existential, authentic on every level! [*laughter*]

MH: Georges, let's just do this. Save your ruminating for the interview. Now sit in the chair and look out of that damn window, will you!

GP: Ok, but let me propose something a little different. Why deny the reader this magical vista of contemplation? Why not invite the reader to see what I see when I look out from my window?

MH: But Georges, this is an author's picture… You have to be in it!

GP: Yes, I will be in it, but I want to be… IN it… the world, where the dog takes the shit, where the air is cold, where the city is loud, in that vista that I never 'contemplate' because I'm too busy writing to look out of the damn window! Let this window be my page, Maurice, it will hold me, trap me inside its frame. I will not tilt my fucking chin and look wistfully away. No! I will look into my readers' eyes and I will say, 'I am you, I am part of the world too, today it is cold and my view is boring, but here I am in it with you. We are together. The reality of writing is not 'contemplative', it is a deeply… uncomfortable experience.'

[*He turns his back to look at the window.*]

GP: I will go outside now, and you will take my picture.

II. A Silent [ ] Overlapping

Inside the table, two inlays of smoked glass are set within a thick oak frame. The shiny aspiration towards elegance locates it in the 1990s, when it was bought in a daze from a vast outlet on the outskirts of town. Its crude unvarnished underside presses down on thighs uncomfortably, concealing inside its frame yet more leaves of wood and smoked glass. This table sits by the window of an empty tenement flat, rented to escape the ongoing battle with entropy at home, where apple cores decay behind cushions, where dinosaurs wait forlorn inside a toilet roll, where the sounds of yelping and outrage prevail.

The dark glass makes a mirror out of this table which holds a singular reflection of the window above. This is a place of silent overlapping. Writing on a mirror makes language a slippage between floating and drowning. The struggle is irrelevant, yet the process of dislocation is pleasurable, like falling when it momentarily feels like flying. Attempts to surface, to hold onto the horizon line, turn the writer's body into a giant eye bobbing up for breath. This eye fixes on unstable vistas: people falling down drunk, a lone man shouting, his chest puffed out and penis exposed, an inside-out umbrella flayed bare on tarmac. At times, the writer overhears a conversation between two people oblivious to being observed, and the indulgence of a man saying, 'we're fuckin' doomed,' to another while laughing. On the street, there are no mouths left anymore, the words spoken on the pavement are hidden behind breath-damp fabric made from old pillowcases.

This glass table reflects nothing of the street's activity, only the window which chooses to frame what it deems important to the writer, namely: the sky, its clouds and birds, fragments of architecture, the crown of a tree.

III.   Without Etymology [ ] Limerence

I think of Baladine Klossowska as I look out from my window. She is most known as the mother of the painter Balthus and lover of the poet Rainer Maria Rilke, who called her by the pet name *Merline*. Her birth name was Elisabeth Dorothea Spiro, born in Germany to a Jewish family in 1886. She moved to France in pursuit of a career as a painter and illustrator, and it was there that she also married, divorced, was a single-parent and lover to Rilke who has since determined her legacy by framing her eternally within a window – his window. Baladine is confined by Rilke within a perpetual state of longing, of sublimation, of limerence – a word without etymology.

In 1924, Rilke produced a small collection of poems titled *The Windows,* which reflected on evenings spent with his beloved Merline in quiet conversation looking out from various windows. Baladine (I will use the name she gave herself) illustrated this collection of poems, published a year after Rilke's death in 1927. Baladine's etchings reveal women often contained by a window, as if lost in a trance. One woman fixes her hair, detached from the act; another woman rests with her hands on the windowsill, looking absently off into the distance; another woman (or are they all the same woman?) sprawls naked on a daybed.

When searching for images of these illustrations on the internet, Google prompts further associated search terms in the following categories:

    de Rola
    Rainer Maria
    Rilke Balthus
    Pierre Klossowski

> far away
> Elisabeth Dorothea Spiro
> Her son
> Her lover
> Her son
> Her husband
> far away
> Her child self

This is how we are to know Baladine. The [online] window to her frames her so, as seen but never known. She has become the women she illustrated: tranced and somewhat deactivated, yet still performing desirability. Between Rilke's words and Baladine's roaming lines, they are neither inside nor outside, but somewhere between, sealed together – a dead fly trapped in the airless vacuum of the double glazing.

Years later, in 1933, her son Balthus completed a painting titled *Window*. It depicts a woman backed against an open window, one hand bracing the sill, the other raised in terror. Against her dark hair is a scarlet headband, her lace-trimmed puff-sleeved blouse has been torn open to reveal a naked breast rigid to the painting's centre. The woman looks upward and to the left of the frame, like an image from a pulp novel cover. Behind her, windows in the building opposite look back vacant. They are only a few metres away yet feel distant, abandoned, blank. With her tight skirt, her exposed breast and dainty little shoes, her bare midriff and childish foreshortened hand, she is both sexualised and vulnerable. The window allows us to imagine her impending fall. Balthus, who as a child watched his mother Baladine wait at her window for Rilke to appear, has invoked this aperture and used it once again to trap and control the narrative of limerence.

Later, the model who posed for the painting reported that Balthus wielded a knife over her while she posed. The long uncomfortable hours holding her position by an open window were frequently interrupted when Balthus saw his model relax enough to adjust her neck or stretch out an arm. It was then that he reached for the knife that lay next to his brushes and raised it high, screaming, *I'm going to rape you, you pathetic little slut*.

IV.   House of [One Thousand] Eyes

The Beige Man

is only ever seen carrying a polythene bag that is inside out. I call him The Beige Man as this is the only colour he wears. However, The Beige Man has successfully demonstrated that there is indeed a spectrum within the beige colour wheel that is both varied and surprisingly nuanced.

He has a small frame with a slight curvature of the spine, a clean-shaven face the colour of cooked trout flesh, and he is balding with a thin line of grey hair above each ear. He walks leaning towards his toes as though on the brink of falling forward. Once I saw him on his front steps talking with his brother and sister-in-law. His brother is a well-respected writer, whose demeanour suggests he is the older sibling. He gesticulates openly when they converse, and I only ever hear the writer speak (he writes in the Glaswegian vernacular). The Beige Man never speaks other than the odd word, but he seems to communicate sufficiently in nods and facial gestures. According to its bulk, his inside-out bag appears to contain small items, maybe a wallet or keys but never groceries, although yesterday he was carrying a bottle of bleach, but the inside-out bag was nowhere to be seen. Perhaps he wanted to disinfect his surfaces – was he expecting a guest? This would be highly unusual, more so now that this is not a government-sanctioned activity.

His curtains have remained unchanged in the fifteen years I have lived opposite. They are a faded rose colour and are consistently neither fully open nor fully closed. I have never seen him look out from his window.

Four Young Girls

sitting kerbside are all wearing: short shorts, tank tops, white Nikes, long hair. They are the sisters who live on the terrace opposite. I saw them once in their lobby when guising with my children on Halloween. Each girl sat silent and blood-soaked, holding sweet-filled skulls on their laps: I admired their dedication to character. Now it is summer, and they have emerged long-limbed and blanched in the midday sun, each holding a smartphone and using it as a camera to pose for selfies. Their most repeated movements include: hands on hips, tilted jaw, mouth open, hair flicked from one side to the other, dipped chin, pouting.

Each movement pivots on the axis of an outstretched arm. The shift from performance to self-scrutiny is disconcertingly abrupt. Following a small discussion, they all prop their devices against a low step, stand back and in unison perform a synchronised routine. On seeing the four phones capture the routine, I lift my own phone to also record this moment.

Score for the Smartphone:

1. Flatten hands like swords.
2. Skim the jaw with a deft slicing motion; elbow leads this movement.
3. Cock head left then right.
4. Toe in, then out.
5. Knees open, knees close.
6. Point both arms down to make the letter 'v'.
7. Fingers form into wolf sign.
8. Retrieve and scrutinise.
9. Scroll. Pause. Finger pinch. Scroll. Pause.

I thumb Insta open and post with the words 'street dance'. I see an unseen story ringed in red. It's a poet I follow with rats on her face, her jaw tilted up. She looks good with rats on her face.

Man, Alone

walks his dog three times a day. Early in the morning, as his dog Sharik (I've heard him call to it) is sniffing along the kerb on the terrace opposite, I watch him stand motionless, staring into the thicket of trees and shrubs that separates the terrace from the pavement of the main road. The curve of the terrace rises around four meters higher than the main street so that the residential part is separated from the commercial side by a raggedy line of lime trees. I often see men disappear into this threshold of trees and trash to piss; few make any attempt to conceal what they are doing and often emerge with their genitals still exposed. The man decides Sharik has nosed this particular pavement for long enough and begins to pull him away. Sharik refuses to budge and seems stuck on a scent of extreme importance. *That's enough, Sharik!*, the man barks as though giving an order. He is deftly ignored. The man then bends over Sharik, staring with a searching look into his eyes and unexpectedly strokes the dog's head gently. Sharik, grateful for this kindness, rolls onto his back, his pink belly and little tufty penis say, *I'm yours*. The man strokes Sharik along his stomach with his gloved hand, he mumbles softly to him, and they both are lost in this intimacy of soothing and cooing and panting. As the man stands up, Sharik flips onto his paws. *Okay now?* the man asks. Sharik seems to nod and decisively relinquishes *the extremely important scent* in favour of pleasing his master as they walk on together. With his muzzle raised appealingly, Sharik maintains eye contact with his master.

V.   Poem as Window [Frame]

Window shopping with Clarice Lispector

On Avenida Copacabana she is seen, looking into a shop window. The writer José Castello approaches to greet his friend. Later he remembered:

> it takes her a while to turn around
> she doesn't move at first, but then
> before I dare repeat the greeting
> she turns slowly
> as if to see something frightening
> and says
> *so it's you.*

At that moment, horrified
I notice that there is nothing in the shop window
but undressed mannequins.
But then my silly horror becomes a conclusion:
Clarice has a passion for the void.

VI. Choreographic Score [for] a Window
     (A Sigil for the Street)

[ ] Go to the window with the most light or that frames the most external activity.

[ ] Observe this scene from your window. Practice shifting focus between what is inside and what is outside.

[ ] Imagine your window as seen from the outside: what is visible, what is not.

1. Detect a rhythm. Select a movement which is not a necessity of propulsion.
2. Repeat this movement slowly three times.
3. Remember a time when you waited for someone at a window – trace their name in the air.
4. Repeat this air writing till you establish eye contact with another person/creature.
5. When eye contact is made, freeze.
6. Imagine yourself as that person/creature.

THE TELLING OF THE TABLES

INT. LIVING ROOM - 4PM

WORK DESK is a dark and lean made-to-measure unit. On the surface she has a busy utilitarian air, yet in close proximity exudes a base scent that is both deep and resinous. She is careful about what she can accommodate, only holding onto the things she deems useful. 'Useful' is defined by the economy of her situation, the available space given to the excavation of her interior life and the functions of evidencing this. Work Desk's folly is to write the world as though from the world's perspective, yet the more she writes the more she destroys it. While she strives for structure, in reality her process is accumulative, messy and fragmentary. Unknowingly, Work Desk thrives in the inanimate richness of this contradiction.

Work Desk is busy typing:

"Umwelt theory states that the mind and the world are inseparable primarily because the mind interprets the world and not the object under observation. In contrast, Innenwelt refers instead to the 'inner world', suggesting the interior experience that accompanies the 'I'"...

A child of around seven years old approaches and
repeatedly taps Work Desk.

> WORK DESK
> (abruptly, almost shouting)
>
> Yes?
>
> > (takes noise-cancelling
> > headphones off)
>
> Oh sorry, my love. Don't you remember
> that when I have these big headphones
> on I'm working...

Regretting her tone, Work Desk takes the child's hand
in hers.

> WORK DESK
>
> Imagine you are on a ship or a plane,
> and once it is off and moving on its
> journey, you suddenly jump off - that
> wouldn't be good, would it?
>
> > (pauses and looks imploringly
> > into her child's eyes)
>
> Well, this is what it's like when I'm
> writing – being on that plane - do you
> understand, my love?

CHILD ONE
(hesitant at first, then wide-eyed)
So... if you stop writing, you will die?

WORK DESK
No! No, not in real life but maybe
in... feeling. On my plane, it's a place
of silence but a very loud silence...

Child One LOOKS SIDEWAYS to the TV.

WORK DESK
...and to make the silence less loud, I
write. Do you understand?

CHILD ONE
Hmm... Mama, your plane sounds scary.
You shouldn't be on that plane.

WORK DESK
Sorry, love, I'm not explaining myself
very well.
(looking anxiously
at the screen)

So, what was it you wanted to ask me?

                        CHILD ONE
            Can I make a tornado in a bottle?
            I need dye, and a bottle and glitter.

INT. BEDROOM - JUST BEFORE DAWN

BEDSIDE TABLE ONE and BEDSIDE TABLE TWO are sororal
twins. Like inverted commas, their function is
to report, open and close on thoughts and times
remembered. Like most twins, they seem to communicate
telepathically - an intimacy which at times is not
as advantageous as it sounds. Their incursions
into the passive reveal unending multiple focal
points conjured, which seem to provoke existential
rumination. They share a languorous quixotic
character, though Bedside Table One is the more
emotionally volatile of the two. Things spoken and
things imagined provide an exhaustive distraction
from their true purpose, which is primarily to
construct the doubling of time and to illuminate the
space between them.

A languorous, unfurling murmur of intertwining voices.

                    BEDSIDE TABLE ONE
            ...what other territories will this
            muteness bring?

BEDSIDE TABLE TWO
I suppose muteness eventually brings words.

BEDSIDE TABLE ONE
...and?

BEDSIDE TABLE TWO
To me, it seems the world is... words. Without words, I expect we'd be lost.

BEDSIDE TABLE ONE
But without words we'd be closer to the truth of things, as we are in the dream world.

A ruminating silence, then Bedside Table One continues as if her thoughts are suddenly made audible.

BEDSIDE TABLE ONE
Words! I mean, aren't they just tools, things to be utilised when a job needs doing? Alone in their cots, syllables are formed, language is a mere playmate - a thing destined to be abandoned when it no longer holds our interest.

                    BEDSIDE TABLE TWO
But...

                    BEDSIDE TABLE ONE
Isn't it just a distraction - a noise?
If it functioned properly, language
would not need words at all!

Bedside Table Two tries to interject, however fails
to get a word in.

                    BEDSIDE TABLE ONE
...before speech and writing appeared,
we all thought intuitively.
                         (sighs)
Let's face it, dear sister, language as
we know it is being skinned alive. Its
death will be slow - but when it comes,
it will have already ossified.

                    BEDSIDE TABLE TWO
         (exasperated yet suddenly energised)
...but what about the pleasure of it!
A world without words is a desert. No
ideas would grow, love would stagnate,
poetry wouldn't exist, it would be the
end of all art!

BEDSIDE TABLE ONE
Would it? What about all the horrors
language brings! The more that is
written or spoken, the more empty
it becomes - language has become
a system of units, placeholders
within an empty network of endless
propositions!

Both fall silent momentarily.

BEDSIDE TABLE ONE
(softly, as though telling
a secret)
I know you know that place where
language escapes... We are speaking
it now. The lingua franca of that
ineffable realm, the shadow world
between us, the locus of our
imaginations, our ideas, our poetry
is ENTIRELY outside language...

BEDSIDE TABLE TWO
Yes, but how does this progress us
in any way, I mean, how can we live
without it?

BEDSIDE TABLE ONE

We listen, we watch, we are quiet.
Silence elongates experience. We must
reject the descriptive and the rational.
In time, our everyday reality will
become... multi-dimensional, then we
will finally know more than we can see.

BEDSIDE TABLE TWO

Can we really exist in the imaginary?

BEDSIDE TABLE ONE

Yes! It may be the only option we have
left.

INT. LIVING ROOM - NIGHT

COFFEE TABLE has a physicality that is both unique and defiantly non-conventional. She is fond of destabilising orthodoxies that she views as both tacit and pervasive. She is known for being disproportionate or 'unbalanced' and is at times avoided for being so. Although she can be exhausting and endlessly rambling, Coffee Table is also sociable, outspoken and entertaining to be around. She absorbs a panoply of information from various sources and believes them all with equivalence. Though her style is not for everyone, her predisposition for thwarting convention positions her as a vector for transformation and change.

> COFFEE TABLE
> When 'trying to make it' as an artist, make sure to get your studio portrait photograph taken when you are at your most depressed. That way you will look skinny, detached and beautiful-sad.
>
> Then, go to your studio and arrange your work in a way that makes it look as if you ARE your work, like it is consuming you. Spread it on the floor,

cover all visible walls and surfaces,
and then allow it to consume you. If
you are a photographer, simplicity
is best: for example, a self-portrait
looking into a mirror, ideally naked or
dressed as a man, for enduring appeal.

In the photograph, make sure you are
either crouching, sitting with legs
tucked under your butt, lying on your
stomach with your hand propped under
your chin or standing awkwardly with
one hand on your hip. If you are
standing, but not sexy-awkward, you may
need to pretend you are making your
art or smoking. Also, remember to smoke
some grass about an hour before the
photographer arrives. Wear something
that gives you a good silhouette,
ideally workwear or something homemade
and slept in.

Importantly, you must not smile - this
will be your future legacy image -
do not fuck it up by looking eager
or like you are on vacation. Aim for
scary-and-complex-sexy not cute-sexy,

one-night-stand-sexy, not girlfriend-
sexy. Other than making art no-one
is interested in at this time, try
to work just as hard on dying before
the age of 40, either of cancer or
addiction. This is key to your future
legacy as an Important Female Artist.

DINING TABLE is strong, well-built and elegant. Her
legs have the specialised tension common to dancers,
her figure (she has three) runs like a parallel
Rorschach, longitudinally across the surface of her
body. She has a charismatic, aloof quality that sets
her apart from others. This perceived haughtiness
is a common misinterpretation of her true nature,
which is of a Highly Sensitive Individual. Dining
Table feels nuance on a sub-atomic level, and she
is continually processing sensory information
unnoticed by most. Her body absorbs and translates
the stories and unspoken secrets that surround
her, and she carries her shadows as well as the
spine that holds her together. Though she finds
noise and chaos overwhelming, she is devoted to
the idea of 'occasion' when she is committed to the
nuanced rituals of conviviality and hospitality.
Such adherence to these occasions can appear as

a narcissistic desire for perfection, a neurotic observance of the rather antiquated codes of etiquette. However, Dining Table is singular in her process of world-making. The narration of her own universe is unassignable to any language other than the resonant frequency of her vibration. She speaks outside these pages.

DINING TABLE

> To those who eat from their knees,
> I say this: the first impulse to be
> present begins with weight. We are
> all objects of the past, yet we can
> really only understand who we are when
> we estrange ourselves from the past
> and see oneself as those inherited
> accoutrements shined and placed on
> fertile ruins.
>
> When a shift is sensed, I spread like a
> cat in the sunshine.
>
> Every cell, every grain, every fibre,
> till space parts my lungs and my
> heart wakes for the potential of this
> weight. This particular weight is the
> weight of future.

I give thanks to my parallel sister
on the floor. Possessing a pious and
enduring strength, my shadow and I hold
each other in place. Despite the abuses,
she is ever-present and always felt in
the dark continent of dust and crumbs.

It's true I perform at surfacing and
all the attendant indignities of 'ice-
breaking'. In gratitude, I sacrifice
my crumbs to her, and she adorns them
as a constellation of jewels.

INT. KITCHEN - 10AM

KITCHEN TABLE is small, bright and practical. Her messy appearance presents her as approachable, dependable and relaxed. Despite her dishevelled look, Kitchen Table is extremely powerful, as she is privy to a matrix of information on individuals, histories, secrets, and fears. Her power, however, is fallow due to the exhaustion of accumulated milk and the weight of unending expectation.

Kitchen Table is constantly arranging and rearranging what she calls 'sub-objects' - things void of meaning, yet she finds these shifting constellations, the migration of things, clusters, split-aparts, spatially gratifying. She is occasionally gifted offerings of flowers, which she holds on to for far too long. For Kitchen Table, the process of decomposition is her only Deity.

Kitchen Table is covered in fragments of paper and miscellanea.

TO DO:

OFFCUTS?
PICK-UP SHOES from
cobbler PRINT OUT
KRISTEVA
SEW SCOUTS BADGE
1.40 - BLOOD
£19.80 ×2
£39.60
6.60
46.20
170.00
= 216.20 till June

Leftovers?

    CLAY
    CHEESE
    EGGS
    SILVER FOIL
    PLASTER
    MILK
    ~~INK~~

INT. LIVING ROOM - 6PM

Work Desk returns to her notebook to notice she was halfway through a word when interrupted. The interruption has dazed her, and as she fails to remember what the intended word was, she becomes increasingly tormented by the loss of the missing word. Child Two approaches.

>					CHILD TWO
>			(holding a pad of lined paper filled
>				with a looping cursive)
>		Mum, are you allowed to start a
>		sentence with 'and'?

Work Table is now experiencing a vertiginous estrangement from her own writing. She is staring at the screen with her fingers over her mouth.

>					CHILD TWO
>
>	Mum!

Any familiarity with her own written thoughts is now suddenly foreign. She stares at the fragmented word started but not finished, severed from its totality, its tautology, its etymology, as a limb severed from its own body. The trauma of its decapitation hypnotises both its killer (her) and the body (the word). These are the hidden silences; the words aborted, deferred, denied. What demanded to be written has just escaped.

> WORK DESK
> What? Sorry… uh, what were you asking?

> CHILD TWO
> (bored of waiting)
> And?

> WORK DESK
> And? What about AND?

> CHILD TWO
> (very slowly)
> Can. I. Use. 'And'. At. The. Start. Of. A. New. Sentence?

> WORK DESK
> Ok, well yes, I mean, why not! It's not really encouraged at your age...

Child Two looks confused.

                         WORK DESK
        ...I mean, teachers probably don't like
        seeing it, but it's really up to you...
        Other conjunctions like 'but' and 'so'
        are a big no-no, but I personally like
        the idea of beginning something with a
        co-ordinating conjunction, as if you're
        joining in on something mid-flow.

                         CHILD TWO
                    (sighs and wanders off
                          mumbling)
        Forget it.

Work Desk turns back to her screen and rereads the
last sentence she wrote.

        Suggesting the interior experience
        that accompanies the "I" (...)

Work Desk has not written the ellipsis following the
'I' – I did (it is there to represent the galaxies of
words lost). Work Desk looks at the blinking cursor
and observes something incapable of returning her
gaze. To sublimate the terror of lost words, she
begins to write in the free-association/automatic
method about the window to her left.

Devoid of intentions for 'good writing', she releases
a torrent of fantasies about transformation.

>   CHILD ONE
>   Mama, can you make me a cut-up apple in
>   a bowl?
>
>   WORK DESK
>   The "I".

Work Desk looks at Child One and then to the loose
foolscap in her hands written almost entirely in
the asemic form, with the exception of one word.
She holds one finger up to make Child One wait, and
with the other types into the search engine, "how
long can the body still continue to propel itself
after decapitation?"

INT. BEDROOM - 6AM

A glass of water refracts the morning light, whispering a transparent flute of light on the wall between them. Lying low to the wall, a small notebook sits on Bedside Table Two, fattened on the ink from a black V Pilot Sign Pen - the only pen allowed for writing dreams.

> BEDSIDE TABLE TWO
> Are you awake? I heard you in the night.

> BEDSIDE TABLE ONE
>
> All night.
>
> Every day an act of birth in this place, it won't stop. The staining is an issue, nothing can be contained in this place.

> BEDSIDE TABLE TWO
> A sign of life at least. We can only ever do so much, hold on to things for so long, at some point we have to let go.

INT. KITCHEN - NOON

Unseen, the preparation and demolition of every day go on, like the inward persistent workings of heart and entrails.

>KITCHEN TABLE
> Today I decided to make a planet.
>
> I arranged everything I would need:
> some yellow vinyl to protect, a bowl of
> water to nourish.
>
> The matter - clay - would need to be
> sizeable for it to behave as it should,
> heavy and almost impossible to control.
>
> At first it was cold and unresponsive
> - refusing to yield to external forces
> but then, with a small degree of
> necessary violence, it began to relent.
>
> As with most things, it warmed with
> the right degree of effort and touch,
> and slowly its packed rectangular
> form of hard edges began to blunt to
> a more spherical shape.

I worked hard for five hours, spinning, rotating, applying whatever laws of gravitational force I could muster. It did not give easily. I wept a little. I paused often to catch my breath and admonish myself for the vanity of such a futile endeavour.

It was then I realised my error: the spherical aspect is only one aspect of a planet, the other is that it needs to orbit. It needed another something to orbit around.

I looked around and found a single egg in a nearby bowl. I placed it on the table next to my lumpen planet.

Immediately, Planet saw Egg and fell in love with it.

Planet gazed profoundly at Egg as if it were the light of an already dead star, knowing that Egg no longer existed but that their meeting was also the birth of Planet's consciousness.

Egg is silent.

Its magnetic presence denuded the kitchen,
it turned the table into a slanted
plane - lemons and apples rolled to the
floor, scattering the cat's dried food
and knocking over her bowl of water.

Planet was helpless to Egg's surety,
sitting there like a paused projectile
in the middle of all this chaos!

Little did Planet know that Egg's
ovoid form was a result of having been
rolled from galaxy to galaxy for so
long, millennia in fact. Of course,
Planet was oblivious to this and to
the mysteries Egg concealed within it.
Planet assumed that, like her, Egg must
be shell all the way through. This
was why Egg didn't see Planet - because
Planet lacks imagination.

Planet, nonetheless, dedicated her
existence to the vision of Egg,
realising that loneliness was a
condition of love.

Her limerence for Egg was of no concern to Egg. In fact, Planet's presence did not even register to Egg, who without doubt had far higher things on her mind - like not getting boiled.

Egg couldn't give two flying hoots about relational theory, gravitational forces, subjectivity, Keppler's Second Law, umwelt theory, the laws of attraction, never mind L.O.V.E!

Sensing Planet had other things on her mind, I took this opportunity to work with her new-found malleability, and soon I was rolling and smoothing Planet into a form simpatico with her weight and inherent edges.

INT. BEDROOM - 7AM

In half-light, the scribbling of notes (rat claws) can be heard. Writing without light does not conform to margins, lines or orientation. The hand in the dark, cartographer of strange continents, hurtles along - a moratorium of thought. It is here that fractured passions, subterfuge, stratagems and therianthropic convulsions begin to separate.

> BEDSIDE TABLE ONE
> I had an awareness of my body, as though seen from another's eyes. I was reclining on a ledge, watching something, a room full of people I think... There was a lot of art on the walls, sculptures protruding from all peripheries.
>
> A man, an artist of some repute with a glinting silver disc around his neck, appeared, and as he spoke, he coiled his body into the shape of my own. Slowly, I was becoming paralysed. A snake emerged from his mouth, flicking the air with its tongue. It weaved towards my mouth, forcing past my

cracked and bloody lips. As I gagged,
I heard my jaw pop.

The curator walked past, the grand
matriarch with bobbed hair and
proprietorial movements. My eyes
cartoonishly pleaded for her to
save me. She stopped and regarded
me as though considering whether to
straighten a painting.

I watched her conclude that my
desperation was not her concern - after
all, the man was an artist of some
repute. Swiftly, she moved to another
room, picking up a tray of amuse-bouche
on the way.

A slow poison spread throughout my
body, and I became trapped under a pile
of classical busts, pearls and onions.
Rats were skittering above my head.
I felt an immense physical pressure,
as though I had been submerged at a
great depth.

Meanwhile, the objects that slowly suffocated me persisted in accruing meaning and becoming heavier and heavier till I was eventually crushed. Once the air in my body had been light, now it was gone, and only the objects that crushed me endured.

I was back on my ledge, waiting for something. I was scared. I was standing on the ledge of an open window. I looked down to the street and observed that my feet were gnarled into deformed pink stumps. Behind me, someone was shouting, 'I'm going to rape you, you pathetic little slut.'

INT. LIVING ROOM - MIDNIGHT

The TV is blaring. Channels are flicked through rapidly.

> COFFEE TABLE
> The land is littered with funky-faced freeeeakazoids! [...] to figure out what the new normal will be [...] restore the rituals [...] the dead are replaced with flags [...] affected by bloating? [...] where the pearlfish curls up inside the sea cucumber's anus sometimes even feasting on its gonads [...] contact tasting [...] contact tracing [...] the Queen is lobbying to conceal her wealth [...] when whitening your teeth [...] Hands. Face. Space. [...] Unprecedented territory [...] WTF do we do? [...] I have a desire for hills in my loft so that I could walk and walk [...]

Coffee Table is hyperventilating, the rectangle emits death at every click. She retreats to a place of silence and begins to write with full caps in black biro.

COFFEE TABLE

1. Call, write, or speak to people you might otherwise see regularly for the specific purpose of uninviting them to your home for a dialogue, hot/cold beverage or meal.

2. Disengage from all friends and family gradually over a year while obeying rules issued by an incompetent governing body.

3. Feed, teach and provide for your family with no income while living in fear of imminent poverty and/or death.

Note: the purpose of this piece is to maintain a sense of normality while providing imaginative responses to the current situation.

INT. BEDROOM - JUST BEFORE DAWN

Locked in a fatal embrace, blood is pouring freely. Bedside Table One speaks as though from a distant world.

> BEDSIDE TABLE ONE
>
> A woman with sand-coloured hair and pale almond eyes is crouched down next to me. She gently takes the rock I am holding and says, What is this? It's just a rock, I say. She smiles and says, Let me know when you know what this REALLY is. Then she starts to strike the rock against the ground. Bang! Bang! Bang! Bang! Each strike releases squirming black insects! They are crawling all over my feet. It is then that I notice they are not insects at all but typewritten letters. There are hundreds of them, all glistening, crawling and clambering over one another. The rock, it seems, is full of words. The woman smiles and says, Now do you see?

INT. KITCHEN - DINNERTIME

A scribbled recipe lies on the Kitchen Table.

INK:
- 1/2 tsp lamp black/charcoal
- 1 egg yolk
- 1 tsp gum arabic
- 1/2 cup honey

Mix the egg yolk, gum arabic, and honey. Stir in the lamp black. Mix paste with a little water. If lumpy, heat will improve the consistency. Too much heat will make writing difficult

>   KITCHEN TABLE
> If you eat it all up, there's pudding
> for after, and please do try to eat
> some of the green things.
>
> Remember granny used to say, looks yuck
> but tastes yum? I know... I know, but
> you have to try. You want to grow big
> and strong, don't you? No, no, I don't
> want to try some - it's all for you.
> How about an egg, a nice egg?

INT. LIVING ROOM - THE DEAD OF NIGHT

                    DINING TABLE
I, an ancient, ask:
what is this surface?

The dust is falling,
greying in degrees.
At times of occasion
I am rubbed in wax
I become useful
I will be smeared
I will be dribbled on
I will be thumped emphatically
I live in the knowledge that
existence depends on utility.

You should know, though
that the glass of water
you are drinking from
is, in fact, my microphone.

INT. LIVING ROOM - 8PM

Work Desk has a book splayed open over her keyboard. She hasn't written for days. She checks her phone, scrolling reels for hours, watching make-up tutorials, dancing children and sleeping cats. She reads Hélène Cixou's 'Three Steps on the Ladder of Writing' intermittently, but her concentration is held only for a minute at a time.

> CHILD ONE
> Can I have something to eat?

> WORK DESK
> You just had your dinner!

> CHILD ONE
> But I'm still hungry. Please can I have cut-up grapes and a bowl of dry cheerios?

Work Desk smooths Child One's hair and smiles.

> WORK DESK
> Okay, okay, let me just finish this... page. But do they have to be cut-up?

Child Two absent-mindedly draws on some typed notes.

> CHILD ONE
> Yes, cuz they're nicer when they're cut
> up, cuz you cut them that way. Why do
> you need to finish the page?

> WORK DESK
> Oh my love, I just need to. One more
> minute, okay?

> CHILD ONE
> But I'm hungry now, Mama.

INT. LIVING ROOM - 10PM

>   COFFEE TABLE
> What do you do on me exactly? You put your stinking feet on me, and your empty head orbits my world. You don't do philosophy on me - you don't even give a fuck about the marks you leave on my body. You think I am over there. But you know what? I'm here, I'm actually here!
>
> That fly that landed on me there? - It's in MY world, and your stupid fucking feet are now in MY world. And this - you ritz-cracker-munching-asshole - is where YOUR world begins to unfold.
>
> You think I am a given - an object, a non-present spectre. You think you know me, you give me a flimsy function, you even gave me a name, a name that is meaningless in every way, even to you.
>
> You wanna know something else?

> I have a background - and it's not the chair or the TV - it's tem-po-ral. It exists in time, that's right - I occupy MY own history, you slackjawed moron! Well, you know what? I am searching for new knowledge, new info, new systems - I'll invent other ways of learning for myself. Yeah, you know what? I quit, I refuse you, I'm dropping out.

INT. BEDROOM - 3AM

> BEDSIDE TABLE ONE
> What are you thinking?

> BEDSIDE TABLE TWO
> Nothing.

> BEDSIDE TABLE ONE
> Nothing?

> BEDSIDE TABLE TWO
> Nothing.

BEDSIDE TABLE ONE
Do you know nothing?
Do you see nothing?
Do you   remember
No   thing?

BEDSIDE TABLE TWO
I'm waiting for the dreams. For everything to be torn apart, for my world to tip over.

BEDSIDE TABLE ONE
What did she say?

'Our bones ache only while the flesh is on them

until the night melts away

until the fury of the night rots out its fire.'

INT. DOMESTIC SPACE

Work Desk is roaming from room to room, searching for something unseen. Frustrated, she only sees the objects that have words assigned to them. 'Table' 'Window' 'Plughole'. She doubts these classifications and dismisses them one by one like unripe fruit. Her frantic searching for some displaced, ineffable fragment has now become the choreography of her dwelling, her searching is not comparable to the way one may search for lost keys or a misplaced phone; it is more akin to eating for the first time - of discovering not just flavour but also the devouring of textures, smells, and form.

                        CHILD ONE

    Mama, can an animal live after being
    skinned?

                          END

In gratitude to: Hélène Cixous, Phyllida Barlow,
Kathy Acker, Fanny Howe, Clarice Lispector, Deborah
Hay, Lee Lozano.

THE SINK IS A PORE

STRAINER	What did she say?
	The voices just can't worm through
	                    Hello Sylvia!
	Perforations keep me from you
	collecting all the words
	unuttered
	while mute
	all those years ago

A cracked egg in the bowl this morning. Its albumen chord coiled stark and shocking against the yolk. Is it still alive? I remember asking my aunt when I was small. That's the strain, she said. It connects heaven to earth. I looked to the strain, hoping heaven would materialise, wondering how it would materialise – inside a golden sun or on the transparent shores of albumen. Much later, I investigated and held a raw yolk in my mouth to get the heaven inside. Slowly, with my skull gentle as a cradle, I rocked my sun, rolling him on the bed of my tongue, until I was without skin. Ripened, he burst from my mouth and rolled down my chin, and the body of Blake was formed. A harvest for tempera! he cried and mixed it with his carpenter's glue and yellow ochre to paint his Mundane Egg.

PLUGHOLE　　　Between inside and out
darkness / light, cyclonic
a single cell, latching on
blind, in the dead
of the night.

       Gestalt   tethering
       drip drip drip
       reality is built
       in the dark

       the metallic taste of a cavity —
       a swallow hole
       watch here while
       all disappears

The studio I once kept had nothing on its walls except for one dog-eared image. I carried this image – a folded sheet of newspaper – to every studio I had till, eventually, I had no studio and putting it up on the wall of my home seemed out of context. The image was of an urban sinkhole in the Japanese city of Fukuoka. The hole and its ruined slope spanned the width of a five-lane street. Shops and banks suddenly devoid of pavements slump lantern-jawed in silence. The street is empty, and a thin air seems perceptible as a remnant of the sudden collapse. The chasm (where no thing gleams) has exposed the innards of the city: its pipes and armatures, arterial networks of tubes and funnels, its dust and mortar, the dermal strata of brick and tarmac. Remnants of brightly coloured tubing fall limp into a gurgling pool of murky dishwater. The sudden exposure of infrastructure, both magnetic and terrifying, appears as though the land has recoiled in horror at a city built on consumption.

TAP   a spigot, a pharynx ?
            or a glistening silver gullet
            information filters
            from aqueducts
            wide as lunar craters

            once more, a fermentation:
            dreaming in
            vitro

I borrow money to take a train to go to the meeting. Save your travel receipts, the curator says, we'll process them for you at the end of the project. Thank you, I say, but would it be possible to advance me some funds now, so I can buy the tickets before the project ends. Seriously?, the curator laughs.

BASIN   Scrying is the ignition, a ritual
for oneiromanic vision and a soapy
little vanishing.

We work on the supposition of debris
as a system: of thinking as a debris as
a system without thinking.

In the evening, scrying
at our sinks, slowly removing
all that we know, humming as we go —

we respect nothing!
we believe nothing!
I embody *no-thing*!

Named as *voiding*, it was taught
from our mothers
who said, to survive, seek places
without any stories.

My friend put her head in a sink to read poetry. She made the sink herself from fibreglass, and I wrote the poem. The sink is like a skull, I said, like the boundary to an unseen infrastructure. I said, look at this spaghetti strand coiled in the sinkhole, imagine it's umbilically connecting us to a network of others standing at their sinks. All this talk of umbilicalism leads us to talking about bathing our babies in the kitchen sink for the convenient and coterminous experience of water. A lot of things are dreamed into existence at the sink, I say. Maybe it's the water, she says, after all it is a floating space.

COMPRES- Gemeinschaft
SION the two of us whisper
COUPLING asleep on the pillow
we know each
other in echo

in the dark, compressed with fear
the bee-dark thoughts
we meld our selves
somehow, to
gether

Some experiences cannot translate into language. Love, trauma, birthing, dying are replete with similes that cause infinite frustration and despair:

like
it was like
like a
like an

This, a language diluted, serves only to wean us gently into nothingness. As a child, my failure to talk for three years was a liberation from the exhaustive loop of translation: from trauma to the cutaneous and kinaesthetic, emotion and evaluation, intensity and prosody, to the semiotic and cognitive, to lexical and linguistic expression, to concrete language, and finally the word. Silence was not passive but a highly attuned vigilance felt at a cellular level. I cultivated scenarios where I could be both there and not there: in groups, watching TV, haunting the spaces of the home that were free from narrative. These absences were formed in the pre-verbal space, on the ghosted thresholds between what we feel and what we know. It is here that it became possible to inhabit a world without language, where everything was truly and starkly itself.

The child can see a woman dreaming at the sink. In a landscape of utility, where language is smeared with daily use instruction and information, the child learns to look for ruptures, to seek the thresholds for the dreamworld. Going 'there' while being 'here' rehearses the duality residing in the spaces of poetry. The creation of meaning and housework are acts of solitude (but not of the reverie as Bachelard ever experienced) and in cultural opposition to the ascribing of 'value'. Domestic imaginaries converge with reality settings, and the spectres and half-remembered fragments point to somewhere that is both no longer nor yet to happen. In this shadowed place where the production of meaning resides, I enter the silence of women poets trying to find their language.

GASKET   a material seal, between
                   two mating surfaces

between lips and
air
between ideology and
science
leaning in
coughing in faces —
in the name of freedom
whose freedom
?
muzzles, they said
– we burn 'em like books

Skirting the park, I edged past a young fleet wi flesh like hotdogs, eyes burlin
aw Mad Dog. Nae doubt been downing it since noon on the green beach,
I say. Come nightside the fleet go streetwild: eyes aw lollin, jaws gurnin,
movin like some fallen murmuration. The young fleet been longin fur this aw
lockdoon. Some yoking fur blood aye, but maest just aching fur shouldering
the gither in crowd shapes. Copters and pig units circlin deaf loud, choppin
the air shoutin, go to your homes, go to your homes, go to your homes.

SINK TRAP   the silent rhythms of struggle:
Eel is tethered helpless to a ghost
line, Lizardfish is sucking
on a cigarette, Seahorse drags
an anti-bac mask, Octopus has absorbed
a barcode beating hard
inside her opalescent breast.

Blockages known (via Rich and Woolf):
    Problems of contact with herself
    Problems of language and style
    Problems of energy and survival.

A mouth / a secret place to snare / encircle / capture. Here, the trap is a holding space, holding the outside from the inside – cold air, infestations, sickness, strangers, litter, ghosts. Society must keep on the outside, subjectivity must be protected by the inside, where revelations are safely enclosed, where the process of being is gently rounded.

At one time, we slept, ate, entertained and worked from one room. Privacy and the interior did not correlate, we were never free from the intimate knowledge of others. The physical actuality of the city and the home is mutable according to the life(s) led in it. I live in one room still, where a body is divorced from its clothes (the city) and its pores (this sink) connect to all that is exterior. Where we are is here – past the epidermal strata, down through to its deep follicular bulb. This is where the space of memory germinates.

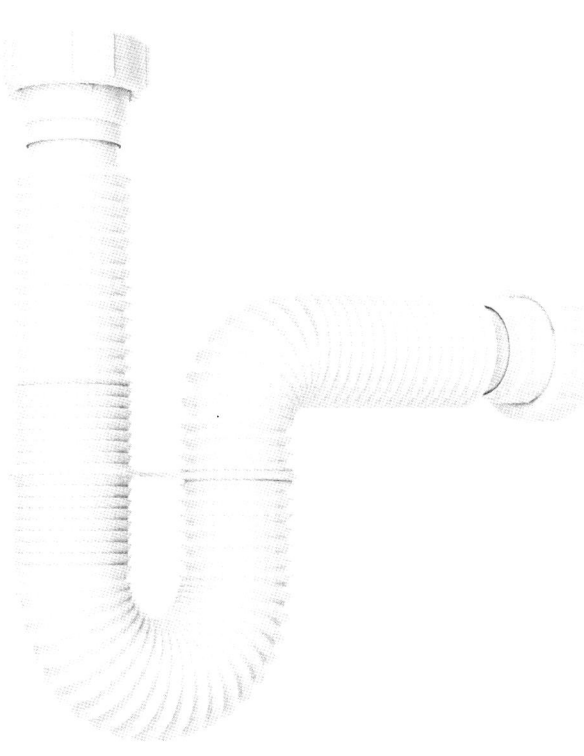

SHUT-OFF VALVE

Here
in this
umbra:
a stillness
punctured
at times by
a heartbeat [drip
drip] means a leak
that takes
me under

I ask —
is this where
I should dwell?
within this space
of rupture
between
tightening and release
here at least
there is
no lingua franca

A READING LIST

- AHMED, S. (2006) Queer Phenomenology.
- BACHELARD, G. (2017) The Poetics of Space.
- BELL, K. (2013) The Artists House: From Workplace to Artwork.
- BENJAMIN, W. (2003) The Arcades Project. Translated by H. EILAND and K. McLAUGHLIN.
- BRADLEY, F. and H. VILALTA (2018) Lee Lozano: Slip, Slide, Slice.
- BRADLEY, F., ed. (2015) Phyllida Barlow: Sculpture, 1963-2015.
- BUSCH, A. (2004) Geography of Home: Writings on Where We Live.
- CAMPAGNA, F. (2018) Technic and Magic: The Reconstruction of Reality.
- CIERAAD, I., ed. (1999) At Home: An Anthology of Domestic Space.
- CIXOUS, H. (2019) Dream I Tell You.
- CIXOUS, H. (2010) Stigmata: Escaping Texts.
- COLBY, G. (2018) Kathy Acker: Writing the Impossible.
- COLLINS, S. (2018) Small White Monkeys: On Self-expression, Self-Help and Shame.
- DARCY, A. (2012) I maginary Menagerie.
- FRANZEN, B., ed. (2013) Phyllida Barlow: Brink.
- FISHER, M. (2017) The Weird and the Eerie.
- HAY, D. (2013) My Body, The Buddhist.
- KOHAK, E. (1996) 'Of Dwelling and Wayfaring: A Quest for Metaphors'. In The Longing for Home, edited by L. ROUNER.
- LISPECTOR, C. (2018) The Complete Stories. Translated by K. DODSON.
- LOZANO, L. (2010) Lee Lozano: Notebooks 1967-70.
- LOZANO, L. (2018) Language Pieces.
- MALLARMÉ, S. (1999) Stéphane Mallarmé.
- MAYER, B. (2017) The Desires of Mothers to Please Others in Letters.
- PEREC, G. (2008) Species of Spaces and Other Pieces. Translated by J. STURROCK.
- PEREC, G. (2020) Brief notes on the Art and Manner of Arranging One's Books. Translated by J. STURROCK.
- PEREC, G. (2011) Thoughts of Sorts. Translated by D. BELLOS.
- PESSOA, F. (2018) The Book of Disquiet: The Complete Edition. Edited by J. PIZARRO. Translated by M. J. COSTA.
- PESSOA, F. (2018) I Have More Souls Than One. Translased by J. GRIFFIN.
- RAINER, Y. (2013) Feelings are Facts: A Life.
- RENDELL, J. (2019) Site-writing: The Architecture of Art Criticism.
- RICH, A. (2000) On Lies, Secrets, and Silence: Selected Prose, 1966-1978.
- RILKE, R. M., W. ARNDT and C. HAMLIN, (1989) The Best of Rilke: 72 Form-True Verse Translations with Facing Originals, Commentary, and Compact Biography.
- RYBCZYNSKI, W. (1987) Home: A Short History of an Idea.
- SADLER, S. (2001) The Situationist City.
- SCHWENGER, P. (2019) Asemic: The Art of Writing.
- SENNETT, R. (2018) Building and Dwelling: Ethics for the City.
- SHONFIELD K. (2000) Walls Have Feelings: Architecture, Film and the City.
- STEIN, G. (1997) Tender Buttons: Objects, Food, Rooms.
- VIDLER, A. (1999) The Architectural Uncanny: Essays in the Modern Unhomely.
- YODER, R. (2021) Nightbitch.

Notes:

The title Site Report references Jane Rendell's *Site-Writing, The Architecture of Art Criticism*, 2010, where Rendell proposes that writing can be the site of building, and thus subject to the same transitions, porosities and critical processes as architecture. Recent feminist discourse in this area has questioned the neutral/distanced tone of theoretical commentaries on urbanism, and *Site Report* attempts to build from this approach, addressing the processes of interpretation that involve an entanglement in the intersubjective and physical spaces of lived experience.

The essay 'Windows', in the first part of this book, features a scene between the writer Georges Perec, the photographer Maurice Henry and the journalist Michel Bosquet. This scene and the unfolding conversation is a work of fiction. All events surveilled in the section 'House of [One Thousand] Eyes' are true, with the exception of the dog's name. Sharik is the name of the dog protagonist in Mikhail Bulgakov's novella *The Heart of a Dog*, 1922.

In 'The Telling of the Tables', each character (table) was inspired by: Hélène Cixous, Phyllida Barlow, Clarice Lispector, Deborah Hay and Lee Lozano.

The Kitchen Table's epiphany in 'The Telling of the Tables', with the egg and the planet, was inspired by 'O ovo e a galinha (The Egg and the Chicken)', a short story by Clarice Lispector.

The work in this book was developed and written during my fellowship at Theatrum Mundi from April 2020 until September 2021.

Thanks:

Enormous thanks to Theatrum Mundi, particularly Marta Michalowska for her trust in my wayward methods, for her careful editing and supportive feedback, John Bingham-Hall for providing this opportunity, Cecily Chua for her enthusiastic support, and Marcos Villalba for his intelligent and intuitive design.

This book is dedicated to my family – Toby, Kit and Robin.

Editor: Marta Michalowska
Concept: Rhona Warwick Paterson
Design: Villalba.Studio
Typesetting: Santiago Confalonieri
Proofreading: Sriwhana Spong
Printing: Grafiche Veneziane

This work is subject to
copyright. All rights reserved.
No part of this publication
may be reproduced, translated,
stored in a retrieval system, or
transmitted in any form or by any
means, electronic or mechanical,
without prior written permission
from Theatrum Mundi.

Copyright
© Rhona Warwick Paterson, 2022

The right of Rhona Warwick
Paterson to be identified as
the author of this work has been
asserted in accordance with
Section 77 of the Copyright,
Design and Patents Act 1988.

Theatrum Mundi
c/o Groupwork
15a Clerkenwell Close
EC1R 0AA
London, UK

Theatrum Mundi Europe
59 Rue du Département
75018
Paris, France

ISBN: 978-1-9161864-8-4

Friends of Theatrum Mundi:
MA Cities, Central Saint Martins
Rudi Christian Ferreira
Catherine Visser
David Chipperfield Architects
Joao Villas

(see https://theatrum-mundi.org/membership/)

This publication is part of
Theatrum Mundi Editions, a series
reflecting current streams and
new directions in our research,
led by our team and collaborators
and shared with our members.
Editions are generously supported
by the Friends of Theatrum Mundi.
Every effort has been made to
trace copyright holders and
obtain their permission for the
use of copyright material. The
publisher apologises for any
errors and omissions and would
be grateful to be notified of
any corrections that should be
incorporated in future editions
of this book.

www.theatrum-mundi.org